I0560587

Everything I Felt, I Wrote

Everything I Felt, I Wrote

Caitlin Austin

Everything I Felt, I Wrote
© 2025 Caitlin Austin
ISBN: 979-8-9987811-2-4

Published by Youth Writer's Press
Colton, California
youthwriterspress.com

First Edition, 2025

All rights reserved. No part of this publication may be reproduced, distributed, or transmitted in any form or by any means, including photocopying, recording, or other electronic or mechanical methods, without the prior written permission of the author, except in the case of brief quotations embodied in critical reviews and certain other noncommercial uses permitted by copyright law.

To request permissions, you may contact the Publisher at
info@youthwriterscamp.com

Printed in the United States of America.

Cover design by Caitlin Austin & Emily Anne Evans
Layout design by Emily Anne Evans / Photon Moment LLC

For the time,
that gave me a chance to heal.

Contents

Everything
I Felt, I Wrote

My Waters

I am something so shallow as a twin,
A daughter,
A dancer,
An actor,
Barrely diving into the surface,
My surface, this is who I am.

While I am all of these things,
I have more deep within my waters,
My deep, dark waters,
Where no one, not even myself,
Are able to swim.
Who I am is sunk under the weight,
Under the waters of who I want to be.
I want to be perfect.
A flawless, unattainable ideal,
I know this much.
This idea of 'perfection' is so unrealistically, me.

But as I dive into my deep, dark waters
Struggling to see the sand
I know is somewhere down there
I find imperfect me,
Bubbling up to the surface
Calling,
Begging,
Pleading to breathe.
It's suffering— suffocating really.

But the way I look,
The things I feel,
They are not flawless, perfect me,
Not the one I feel I need to be.

So let it rain.
Let the water fall from the sky
And send ripples to disturb my perfect surface
For only the moments it rains,
For only the time it takes the clouds
To send back the water they carelessly take,
Will imperfect me be allowed to see the surface.

And just when the clouds
Have nothing else to give
Will my imperfect self
Be shoved back into my sea.
My ocean.
My deep, dark waters.

The clouds gave me back
The weight I so needed
To keep my secrets so deeply hidden.
Because no one is to see
That underneath my surface is a mess.
A sandy ridden mess.
And no one shall see the life that swims beneath
Because my coral is broken,
Shattered to bits.

And so,
The ripples will faded
As though they never existed before
Because perfection,
Unattainable perfection,
It takes hostage my imperfections.
There is no room in 'perfection' for imperfection.

And imperfect me knows its place
It's unreachable place.
And though it doesn't want to
It fades to the depths of my sea.
My deep, dark, unswimmable sea.
And it only flounders,
When it feels it can't breathe.

Snowman's Name

I don't know how I got here,
Standing with my fists clamped in a ball
Frozen with unruly fear,
I am standing in a disaster filled hall.

My favorite brown picture frame
Is shattered on the ground
And my snowman, I've forgotten his name
He is nowhere to be found.

I don't know what occurred
But I'm sure I'm to blame.
It is nowhere near absurd
To say I am desperately ashamed.

Perhaps I was blinded by rage
Anger always works in odd ways.
Perchance I was in a saddened stage
But I don't think it was a sad phase.

I suppose all there is now to do,
Is to clean up my mess and learn the snowman's name
And after an hour or maybe a few,
I'll get this hallway looking the same,
maybe even brand new.

My Little Prey

I sit in the corner of this room
Waiting, always waiting
For my next prey,
Meal, I like to say.
This time it has taken them a while
For then to show their pretty little face,
But they will,
They always do.
It is just a matter of time,
So I'll patiently wait.

But when they appear,
I know just what I'll do.
I'll tie them up with a stick web of rope
And I'll watch them submit
Knowing there is no escaping,
And absolutely no hope.
And then I'll work slowly from their gut up
I'll start with their stomach and their liver
And I won't stop until I get to their heart.
Yes, I know just what I'll do
When they finally show up.
And they will, and I will play my part.
...

I never thought I would walk
Where my body was already outlined with chalk
But I did today

I thought I'd have more time before my end
But I suppose, I do not.
If only I had known,
About the predator looking for prey,
I believe I would have felt, way less betrayed.

...

Finally I see it,
My meal, my game
I won't pounce now
I'll let her think she's safe.
She'll lock herself in a small little stall
I'll sit here and I'll wait.
Every prey is remarkably the same.
They'll see their predator
And still look for an escape.
Unfortunately for her, I stand by the only one.
There is only one way to run,
Nowhere to hide, absolutely none.
She come back eventually.
And I'll be here when she finally does.

...

I should have known to run
I felt its dark presents
From the moment this had begun,
Even before I had seen what it had really done.
But when I stepped out of the stall
That's when I knew my life would be gone.

...

Finally, its all I have been waiting for,
But wait, what's going on?
Water? Soap?
Where have I gone?
To heaven?
To up and beyond?
In heaven does food prepare itself,
Because here, it certainly does.
She's washing herself for me,
Awe, I am so touched.
How sweet really.
I have eaten my prey dirty before,
But I suspect this one will be a treat.
Just hurry so we can finally meet.

...

The moment I had realized I wasn't alone,
Was the most horrendous moment
I have ever known.
Something was waiting for me all this time
I had no idea, and no excuse as to why.
I was oblivious,
And so now I have no choice but to comply.

...

My prey is mine.
She spots me,
But a reaction I am not familiar with conspires.

She first stands frozen.
As if she was a tv and I had just paused it,
She stands there knowing she has been chosen.

Then she walks back and forth
As if she is racking up a mile.
I offer her my wicked smile,
And I don't think she liked it.

Is she mumbling to herself?
This has never happened before.
But just when I think it is done,
She bends to my level
Looks me in the eyes
And she begs.

...

What else was I supposed to do
When looking death right between the eyes?
I wasn't going to put up a fight.
I wasn't going to stand up and cheer,
No, I fear what is before me here.

...

But if freezing, pacing, mumbling or begging
Weren't enough
Add crying to the list.
I have never seen prey so fragile like this.
Typically they stand proud
And fight till the very end,
But this one
This prey
This prey does not.
It confuses me
And 'I am sorry,'
That is all I have to say.

...

I am trapped today
And there are no escapes.
No one knows I am here,
That may be for the best.
No one I love will be here to find my remains.
But maybe I'll try one last cry.

...

There has never be a prey I let loose
None are here to attest.
I eat what I set my hopes on,
And this one here,
She was my next meal.
But I don't think I can.
After all, I've made her cry.
This was never my goal.
And it's not just one tear either,
I've pulled a river from behind her eyes.
So I think that this time,
I will let her go.
There is always more food
But this one doesn't deserve to die today
It's too fragile to enjoy,
So goodbye my little prey.

You're All Wrong

You're all wrong.
You talk too much.
You can't even sit still.
You can never remember.
I suppose I am all wrong.

How many times can a person
Hear these complaints about them
And still come back as them?

It's my fault.
I actually believe that my talking
Isn't annoying to others around me.
I could ramble for hours on a topic
No one but I care about.

I'll use my last words to scold myself
Then, I'll yank out my vocal cords,
So I don't have anything more to say.

It's my fault.
I have this leaking water bottle of energy
Stored inside of me,
I have to get the energy out somehow
So I'll rock until I make others dizzy.

I'll screw the lid on the leaky bottle,
And I pray and hope that after a while,
The bottle will not explode.

It's my fault.
I can't remember anything
My brain dumps out all the things I need
Even my childhood is gone
Except from one simple memory.

I'll trade the one memory for a working brain
All so everything I will be able retain
So no one can say, 'Why can't you remember anything?'

It's my fault
I will change, I promise,
But if I succeed,
Can I have your guarantee,
That you will finally love me?

On Its Own

My pencil used to write on its own
It's lead was always taken care of
The erase was always new.
It's wood was always straight
And it always looked brand new.
It's font was so pristine
And every word was spelt right.
It takes pride in how it looks
And especially in what it writes.

Something changed.
Something is always changing these days.
My pencil became everything it was not.

It showed up late to work
And it stopped writing on its own.
Its lead was tattered
And the eraser disappeared.
The wood developed a significant curve
It even looked old and dead.
Its font was jagged and crooked
Every word was misspelled and nothing looked good.

What happened to my pencil?
What changed it so?
My pencil became everything it was not.

My pencil sat me down,
To have a little talk
And the tale it told me,
I could not believe.

"Someone tried to tell me what to write."
Everybody knows my pencil is always right.
"But when I said, no, they forced me
Even as I begged, please."
Oh poor pencil,
My heart bleeds.

"They got what they needed
And finally let me be."
Oh what a relief.
"But when I picked myself back up,
I simply didn't believe,
That there was anything else for me."

"They tried to tell me who I should be,
What I should say.
They dug my tip into the page
And they used up my eraser.
They wrote sloppily,
And misspelled even their name,
I was no longer Pencil,
Writing on my own."

"I have no more to write,
I have lost my inspiration
I find no delight in what I should write.
I tried.
But, I'm lost with no end in sight."

"Will I ever be able to write?
Will I ever be good enough?
Someone felt they had to tell me how
And what I should write."
Poor pencil, it lets out a howl.

"I suppose I'll retire,
And put the pencil in me to sleep,
For I was not good enough.
Oh, please, just let me be."

My poor pencil.
It no longer can be,
The pencil who writes
Not even on its own.

My Jailers

I suppose fear is lighting the way,
Stress is coaxing me in,
Anger is fueling my steps
And all three of them are leading me away.

They fill my head
With its carefully crafted lies
Ones meant to distract me
From the purpose of life.

Am I supposed to be enjoying the journey?
Because it is joy I have left behind.
I am carrying what's left of my pride
And my fragilely crafted mind.

The three of them lured me in
With the promise of comfort,
A home I have never been given,
And to them I was driven

I thought at first
It was odd to draw me in
Just to freeze me out,
But I guess that just the fun
Of being the jailers no doubt.

Of course fear starts it all off.
It whispers to me, reminding me

That I shall never see the light again.
I'm its prize, and fear will never let me out.

The weight of its presents
Is enough to keep me tied to the floor
And though to it I am not bound,
I can't find it in me to leave the ground.

But torture doesn't stop with fear,
No it is only the beginning,
The introduction, nudging the prisoner,
Towards the ledge of the abyss.

Stress is the second act,
It starts off the game.
The one I should welcome,
For I am the one it plans to tame.

Stress doesn't work on its own,
I am too much to take,
Instead it works with fear
Until my legs begin to quake.

I am still on the edge of the abyss,
And as I stand there, my heart begins to race.
For it is stress amplifying my fear,
Reminding me, I am about to fall in.

But it is anger that does me in.
It comes at me with a force I can't reckon.
And as I fall back, it is then I realize,
This was never where I wanted to end.

You see I was on a straight and narrow path,
My directions were all locked in,
And happiness was in sight
When I allowed them to draw me in.

Happiness is always a trap,
Because just when I think I am there
I have fallen into the attack,
There is no rescue or chance to take it back.

My jailers caught me by surprise
And I allowed myself to be held at the knife.
For I could have fought,
But I allowed myself to be caught.

And as I fall into this abyss,
The darkness swallowing me whole,
My jailers were smiling down at me,
While I was too busy with my fall.

Poor Bug

How could we hate something yet pity it so?
It is like a bug in our house.
We know we must kill it— because we hate it.
It is an insistent bother.
A reluctant pest.
Miserable, really— to live with a bug in our house.
So we hate it, and do everything within our power
To hunt and kill it with little remorse.
We send out the rivalry and call in the commanders.
There is no room for playing games.
We come armed and ready for war.
We will not stop until,
The threat of an insect is finished and left in dust.
It is easy to talk.
Simple to give orders.
Nice to never have to look
The enemy in the eyes, and watch the light
The shimer,
The hope,
Fade from their eyes.
Perhaps it is easy to kill something so small,
Because its eyes are so tiny
Invisible, really.
They can only be seen under a microscope,
The microscope none of us have.
Maybe if we all could see their eyes,
We wouldn't hate them so.

But I've gone to kill a fly,

An ant,

A beetle,

A bug.

I have gone to kill the things I hate,

With a carefully curated plan,

I thought so important to make.

And I should feel full, exhilarated, and proud.

I have come so far.

I am facing off to my enemy, my foe.

But instead of full, exhilarated, and proud, I feel evil.

Pity's doing.

I hate the thing so— I hate the bug.

The bug should die.

It has no right to walk into my home,

To occupy my home.

It has no right.

Yet I feel evil having to put its body into the ground.

I feel pity and sorrow for the bug— the bug I can't smash.

Maybe it didn't mean trespass.

Perhaps it is begging for its life I am about to have.

I am standing over the bug and all I can do is imagine.

It has a family to fly home to.

A colony to feed.

A queen to serve.

Yet with a single motion.

One single decision,

I can make it disappear—

The bug disappear.
And though the bug has no right to step out of line
Trespass, invade, break a law so to say,
I can't bring down the swatter.
I can't send out the bleach.
I can't command the army to defend.
I just can't do it because the poor bug,
The bug I pity— it has a life of its own.
And how dare I think of taking it away
Simply because I hate it.
But it is just a bug after all.
Just a nasty,
Gross
Unloveable.
Repelling bug,
To most people, it's nothing worth pardoning.
But is death too cruel?
I hate the bug.
Everything in me tells me to smash the bug— kill it.
But my heart,
My foolishly kind heart torments me.
I can not do what my body wants,
What everything in me wants me to do,
Begs me to do.
I can not kill the bug because I pity it.
How could I hate something oh,
So much yet pity it even more?
What does this say about me?
That I can't make up my mind?
That I am so out of tune with my emotions,

That I care so much for a bug?
I suppose there is more I both hate and pity,
But standing over this bug,
This fly,
This ant,
This beetle,
This bug.
It's probably begging for my mercy.
Crying for forgiveness— for all it is about to lose
Promising never to commit such a crime again,
I just can't do it.
I no longer stand here,
Feeling sorry for the small creature.
No, my pity shifts to the larger creature in the room.
The one that both hates and pities,
The small, helpless creature on their kitchen floor.
Me.
I hate that I can't make a decision,
And I feel sorry for how much time I have wasted trying.
These two feelings are a painful contradiction,
I have to live with.
Either keep the bug and pity it,
Or bring down my hatred filled hand.
But I think I'll do neither.
Instead, I'll do the unthinkable,
The unimaginable,
The most painfully boring solution.
The solution that satisfies both feelings.
I hate the bug.
It can't stay in my house, and it won't.

So, I'll open the sliding glass door.
And I will kick him out.
But I hope that when he ventured back home,
He makes it back safe and sound.
Oh, what a sad pitiful bug in my house.

Garden of Faults

If you have ever been to the garden of faults
You know just where I am.
Pretty flowers surround even the darkest of souls,
Because here in this garden
Everyone is allowed.

And though everyone is welcome,
Only a few of us actually go.
It is a place so desolate and cold,
You need a winter coat just to cope.
But I have come just as I vowed.

I am keeping my promise to the flowers.
I have come searching for the prettiest ones.
The biggest heaviest ones
The ones I can take home
And stare with pride.

I walk the rough path ahead,
Rocks moving and bouncing
Out from under my long step,
Finally the first flower,
I see it bowing its head.

It knows why I am here,
It knows my heart's goal.
So veering from the path,
I attach my hand to the stem,
And I yank it from the ground.

It is mine,
All mine,
Selfishly mine.
The first flower,
It is in my palm.

But it is not the only one I see,
Surrounding it are more flower,
I start plucking them to my glee.
Flower after flower, the ground becomes bare,
And my hands are so full, it is hard to fare.

With every flower, I wear more,
More weight,
More dirt,
More pain to my tired limbs.
But I must keep picking, because I promised.

I vowed to the flowers that I would return,
And find the prettiest ones,
The heaviest and biggest ones.
I can not stop until they are all in my arms,
And I can look at them proud.

So regrettingly I keep on my way,
The garden of faults keeps such a nice selections
So that not even for a second
Or a moment is there time to catch one's breath,
Or even time to stop.

If only I had someone else with me
To pick the flowers and carry them home.
Maybe then I could get them all,
But my hands are so full, flowers are starting to drop.
I suppose I understand now why not everyone comes.

The weight is so heavy.
I have to stop.
I can't keep this up.
It has to stop.
I can't carry every flower within my arms.

It is impossible.
So I drop the flowers,
And they splatter across the ground,
I feel bad I have picked them,
I made the ground go bald.

I suppose the ground must have felt so happy,
It had less weight to carry.
All the flowers were in my arms,
No longer the ground's responsibility.

But I don't think I can take it
I can not relieve the ground of its weight
Because I would be so tired
Of all the guilt I would have to carry.
Perhaps the garden of faults
Is where the flowers should stay.

Giving Me a Guide

Hello, happiness.
Are you out there somewhere?
Or are you stuck buried in a mine?
Are you playing hard to find?
Are you one big lie?
Can you ever be mine?

Did someone once find you
And bury you back up,
So only they can enjoy,
What they so luckily find?
Are they living a happy life?

If this is the case,
Send out a sign.
Even if you can't be in my life,
I would rather be informed,
And not left in the darkness behind.

Are you a tale we tell our children,
So that they can be hopeful for their future?
Do we tell them you will be there later,
Giving them 'life's great tour,'
And showing them all there is in store?

Do we tell them this so they don't have to fear
The unknown,
The scary,
The adventure about to begin?
Are you there to comfort them within?

I have grown up
If this is the case,
I can handle the truth,
No need to lie to my face.

Are you only available to some people?
Am I one of the lucky souls
Who weren't so fortunate enough
To have you present in their life?
Was it my lack of luck?

Perhaps you choose your favorites
And it is them who you allow to wear
The symbol of your touch.
I know what shoulders you sit on.
It is as plain as day and dawn.

Their lips are pulled and stretched to beyond,
They parade around
Displaying the white bone in their mouth.
We all have it, the bone,
But is it only them good enough to show it?

But regardless, if I am your favorite or not,
I think I know what you feel like,
And when I get a little taste,
My hope sores and I pray
That finally it is today,
That you have shown me some grace.

On this lucky day,
You hold my hand guiding me through life,
And together we float so high, soaring in the sky,
But to my demise
You let go of my hand
And I am picked right from the sky.

Happiness,
I have chased you around
Hoping only to be chosen
But I fear,
It is only leading me closer to my doom.

This time, I am really falling from the sky,
Crashing right through buildings,
Not stopping till I rest atop a thin layer of dust
Protecting me from the
Hot molten lava in the center of our earth.

My skin is scorching.
Too hot, I shouldn't lay there long, but I'm stuck,
I can only stare up the tunnel and wonder,
Perhaps this is where you burn.
In the bright, hot, molten lava.

Do I have it right this time?
If this is how far I have to go to find you,
I think I have gone too far.
Perhaps it was delusional,
To think that you, happiness, would be this far down.

I can say I have gone to the darkest depths
To find you, so called happiness,
But I have returned empty handed,
Burnt to the bone,
And sadder than I can remember.

Perhaps chasing you, happiness,
Only makes the darker, darkest.
Perhaps you, happiness, point out,
All the negative,
And shakes them all about.

Happiness,
No wonder you always win at hide and seek.
You distract us with all the other players
All while you keep changing spots.
I used to try to beat you, win you happiness,
But it's on your team I should have been.

I think I know why I can't find you,
I am too busy looking,
And too devastated when I can't find you.
I understand how to now,
I'm done playing this game.

I don't expect you to walk right out,
Giving away your precious spots,
We'll play this game again,
And you'll need as many as you got.
So for now, I'll climb my way back up.

I'll make it back to the surface,
And return to normal life.
I have nowhere else to hide,
And when you're ready,
I'll be easy to find.

If your not a tale we tell our kids,
If you not buried in a mine,
If your done playing hard to find,
If I could be your favorite,
And your symbol could be mine,
If I am meant to be with you,
You giving me a guide,
You sitting by my side,
You shining the way with light,
I'll wait for you.

So happiness,
If you are reading this,
Hearing this,
Goodbye.

Ripe on My Tongue

It's on the tip of my tongue
It's practically falling out of my mouth
Like a fruit too ripe on the vine
It's hardly hanging on

It is soft,
And juicy.
Plump for the picking
Needing to be harvested.

Yet I leave it on the vine
Hoping that one more day will serve it well,
'It will be sweeter,' I tell myself
But it can't get any more ripe.

It is simply rotting
It'll turn bitter as it always does
And it will be all my fault because
I left it on the vine too long.

Perhaps I should just speak
The fruit off the tip of my tongue
Maybe I would feel lighter
Knowing that it has finally stopped rotting.

But I know it will never happen
I would rather let it rot away
Than to speak what is really on my mind
Because if I do, it might actually be ripe.

It might be exactly what I mean
And it might be delivered so perfect
That everyone around me
Simply turns away.

I hear people say,
The truth is always hard
But what if that is what I raise
On my silly little vine

A little orbs of truth
Waiting until the perfect time
Waiting to shock someone
With how they're simply sublime.

I can't just pick the truth from my vine
I must wait until it is more of a refined design.

It will have been filter too much
Like a watered down coffee.
And then I will give it a slight nudge
And the rotten truth will slide right off my tongue.

Quite Scared

I wish I wasn't so scared.
I wish I didn't see you,
And want to crawl out of my skin.
I wish I didn't have to keep you in my sight,
I hate that I have this fear.

Your not that big,
In fact you're rather small,
But my big fears are so large,
It doesn't make sense
None really at all.

It's not like your reaching out at me
Running after me until I fall.
Your not here to scare me,
But you do.

You don't yell at me cruelly,
You don't jump out and yell, boo,
And you don't threaten to leave me
Or pretend to be a stuck statue doll

Just being yourself,
You managed to leave me
Tucked in a corner
Like a rock solid ball.

You're not even the size of a penny,
Not to make you feel bad,
But can we pause to talk about your legs?
They are thinner than my hair,
Yet longer than it too.

Everything about you makes me uncomfortable
How do you simply enjoy hanging in the air?
You confuse me,
And it is quite insufferable,
When we are alone you leave me in despair.

So I am sorry,
Perhaps you could leave
Ignore me always
Driver yourself away
Enter another universe
Relax somewhere else
Because here in my house
You make me uncomfortable
And most of all scared.

Locked Them Away

Perhaps the only real things
Are the feelings I refuse to feel.
For so long my world has been a buzz
Things to do, no time to lose

So instead of taking time to feel.
I'll shove it all down
Back into my little box.
I'll tighten the lid
So not even I can get if off
And I'll place the zapper into position
That way there is a persistent buzz.

This will work for today
And if I am lucky, tomorrow.
It is not a permanent solution
Nothing is cured with electrocution
But until I find a resolution,
Electrocution will have to do.

Numb is all I have time to feel
Nothing should appear real
Because if it does,
That means there is more to feel.

But the box can only get so full
It can only absorb so much buzzing.

Eventually, it will explode
And the contents will have
Nowhere else to go.

It's only a matter of time
Before all I tucked away
With rise to the surface
And I'll have no option
But to bear the weight of my choices.

They rip and tear
Right through my chest
They won't stop until their in my head
The emotions don't come to play
After all, I am the one who locked them away.

I don't have the right to ask for their mercy
I shoved them in a box
And electrocuted them until they escaped.
I have no choice but to suffer my ill fitted fate.

Like a Cactus

Perhaps like a cactus,
I too stand in the middle of a desert
Far from any source of life
Thriving on my own.

There is nothing but golden sand
To keep me warm on the cool nights,
And the stars are bright.
They're my only companions.

I wish I could say, I don't know how I got here,
But I took the caravan of fear,
And it lead me to the middle,
Middle, of the desert and dropped me off.

Like a cactus I stand
My thorns held high.
You can approach and face danger,
Because only when you get near,
Are you at risk of being hurt.

Or you could stand
From your well acquainted distance
And watch as I grow
Right from out of the dirt.

But I think fear puts me in a difficult spot.
Stuck between reality

And what could be.
Scared of allowing anyone close.

If I become the cactus,
There is nothing to be sacred of
Because there's no life around.
It is only me, the stars, and the sandy dirt.

I can thrive on my own,
No need for anyone close
Because if they are near
I will be swallowed whole.

Just give it some time, you'll see,
I sit, fearing what life could be
When and if humans grow near,
So I request no humans here.

But, eventually a drought will come.
And though I might not need too much water,
A hardy cactus like me will face defeat,
The sun will dry me out.

And I be out here,
All by my lonesome self.
Because I refused to drop the needles
I raised in the direction of everyone else.

I Choose

I choose not to talk,
I choose not to tell you what was going on
These were my choices,
And they lit my way into my cave.

How was I supposed to tell you
What was going on with me,
When I didn't know
About the cave I was adventuring into?

I promised myself
To listen to your advice,
I would find a family somewhere else,
And I found it in the only place I could, myself.

When I decided to venture in,
Shutting my lips as if to block the entrance,
This was my attempt at destroying you,
But it was the process of destroying myself.

At the time, I didn't know,
What shutting you out would do.
It was me and the world,
There was nothing I couldn't do.

My anger for you,
Kept my fire fueled and warm.

And the heartbreak I felt,
Keep me alive just to prove you wrong.

Maybe though, in all the time
It took for me to get it right,
I was proving your point.
Perhaps you were right all along.

I thought if I blocked you out,
You would know you did something wrong.
And if I stopped hanging about,
Sometime I'd hear your apologetic song.

I argued back and forth with myself,
Wondering whether an apology would be enough,
And I have decided, once and for all,
'I am sorry,' will never be enough.

I didn't realize how consuming ager was
Until I ventured in and blocked the entrance.
But there again, these were my choice cause,
I took your advice and found a new family, myself.

Who Would I Be Then?

Should I thank you for who I am today,
Or should I resent you for who you forced me to become?

I stood in front of an invisible barrier
You thought to wisely to put up
Maybe if I had reached out
I would have known I made it all up.

Nothing stopped me physically.
But a silly rule
A harmless mandate
It kept me from getting to you.

Its like I was frozen in time
My feet were glued to the concrete
There was nothing I could do
I could not get to you.

Maybe it would've been different
If you handed me the keys
Maybe I would be different
If you didn't take them with you.

I wouldn't feel so alone
Or feel like I have to
Conquer the world all on my own
Maybe I would be different.

But I didn't reach out to find
That in fact the barrier was a figment in my mind
Nothing trapped me into staying behind
Nothing besides you and your fabricated lies.

Maybe if I had fought,
And had not let your words define me
And instead of asking 'please mercy'
I would be a different, happier me.

If I had believed you didn't mean what you said,
Who would I have become?
If I blamed it on your temper heated words,
Would I still be feet behind the invisible line?

Should I thank you for the tears I cried?
It was just a matter of time,
One day they would have fallen anyway,
Perhaps you just speed up the timeline.

Or should I resent you for the pain?
No one should have to face someone so cruel.
No one should have to hear those five word,
Especially when they've come unprepared to the duel.

If I had been someone other than my forgetful self
If I hadn't spent forever trying to remind myself
What I really forgot in the end,
Would I forgive the person I am?

The five cruel words
They should never be repeated,
Yet is it because of me and who I am,
That there was ever a need for them to be created?

You must have been thinking them for a while,
Because they rolled or your tongue.
It must have been easy to say
Because to your memory my face never clung.

Was my face shocked?
Was I sad?
Did I show the pain?
What emotion did I have on display?

I live behind the barrier
You don't remember you hung.
What hurts me more is its only my memory,
Your words ever haunt.

Your aren't haunted,
Or taunted.
This is not something you can regret
Because it was the first thing you chose to forget.

It's only me.
And how could I choose to forgive you
When for so long I've hated myself
Because of the memory I can not flee.

Who would I be,
If I choose to forget to?
Who would I be,
If I had fought the barrier?
Who would I be
If I didn't have this memory?

Would I like me then?
Would I be a good person there?
Would I not be standing stuck
Behind an invisible barrier?
Would I be able to forgive myself
For the mistake I made?

Who would I be,
If it was this memory,
That I did not keep?

So the question still stands,
Should I thank you for who I am,
Or should I resent you for who you forced me to become?

Where There are Beasts

The concrete comforted me.
It was an odd feeling to say the least.
It pulled me to the ground
And massaged my aching feet
It rocked me back and forth
Until I could finally breathe.
But by that point,
I was sure I could never leave.
The pavement was my new home
My new safe place,
Because it was the one I thought I had to leave,
But leaving, fed me to the beasts.

The concrete always screamed up to me
Never trust the sheep
Because while they are fluffy,
You never know what its coat is hiding
After all, there could be a creep.

It was my mistake really,
I stepped off the concrete and into the dirt.
I found comfort in their flock.
I would have been lucky to find only a creep
But I found a savage full beast.
One with a silver tongue to say the least.

Growl after snarl,
His words come from a dark place.

A chamber locked within the creature's soul
Now that we have come face to face,
I know that I am the key.
I can unlock his chamber,
The chamber, I was foolish enough,
To think he wouldn't have.

I always thought I could tame a beast.
I always thought I was good at that sort of thing.
But it turns out, I was wrong.
Wrong about so many things.
There is no taming this beast
No slaying this monster.

So I stand with my head held high
Proud for the beast,
All so he could knock it down.
And I take his lashes.
And I take his bashes.
And I take his cruelty,
Knowing that it is no fault but my own.

I forgot the most important thinq.
I forgot what the concrete always screamed.
Do not trust the sheep.

And so when I return to the concrete,
The pavement,
It takes me under its nonexistent wing
And when I beg for its forgiveness,
It pulls me in.

It no longer screams,
It only whispers,
'Do not trust the sheep.'
I know this now.

As it pulls me to the ground,
And as it massages my aching feet,
And as it rocks me back and forth
Until I can finally breathe,
At this point
I know I'll never leave.
The pavement is my new home
My new safe place.
Because it was the one I thought I had to leave,
But leaving only fed me to the beasts.

I know now, the dirt is not safe.
And wherever the concrete may lead,
I will trust it.
Because it is the only place,
Where there are no beasts.

Tired of Circles

I think I am finally saying goodbye.
In my life, I have come to the time
Where I am ready to move on.

I have given it enough of me,
Paid it enough mind
I am ready, it is time.

Everyone always say,
The past is in the past.
But I have been living there for some time.

So, I am finally saying goodbye.
I am walking towards my future
And I am done looking back.

I dwell in one moment in my past,
And I allow it to fuel my future.
I am tired of the path it is leading me on.

In circles, that's where I'm headed.
Round and round I go.
Not making progress, but not falling behind.

More like tumbling through life,
Hoping one day I might see the light
I purposefully dim for myself.

I don't want to have to take another right turn.
And I am done walking till I'm dizzy.
I've had enough with circles.

For too long,
I've relived the same moment that brings hurt
All so I could feel pain, a punishment for myself.

But I'm not longer standing in that moment,
On that concrete.

I not watching you leave,
And sobbing where you can't see me.

And I'm not begging to believe
That what you said isn't what you mean.

I'm not there,
That's not my reality,
So why is that all I'm remembering?

I am sitting in a car
Heading to something better.
My future.

And why should I let the past
Stab gouges into my tires?
I need them for my travels.

Why should I allow the past,
To drain my tank of gas?
My car needs it so I can escape.

And why should I let the past
Throw rocks at the windshield?
It protects me from the bug filled battlefield.

I can't go towards the new road
When my eyes are glued
To the rear view mirrors.

So I'll leave the past right where it belongs
It's about time I complete this task.
I am heading for my future,
And I am tired looking back.

Goodbye my memory.
I won't forget you, or forgive that you exist.
But I won't live in you,
Because I'm not in the past.

It Could Without Me

The world could rotate without me.
My family can operate without me.
The life I live doesn't need to exist.
I'm only hanging on because I feel the need to.

I used to sit at the top of my stairs
Listening to the conversations below.
I would sit there and cry
Because I know
Without me, life, it can carry on.

I would watch my life on replay
Like watching a show on purpose
Simply because it made me feel something
No matter how self destructive it was.

I used to believe that I was the issue.
All the problems that my family had,
All the bad times we faced,
It was all because I was there.

And I knew that if I disappeared,
They had a chance at being happy.
It might have taken sometime,
But they wouldn't need me after a while.

I believed I was selfish for wanting to live
To stay in this world and exist,

Because when I was around,
Things would always go wrong.

I was angry at myself
For who I was,
And all my flaws,
'I am all wrong,'
That's what I would tell myself.

I was a monster.
An atrocious human being
Something that should be taken care of,
And dealt with in a brutal manner.

I had no purpose for living then.
I ditched the notebook,
The fantasy world I used to live in,
And the hobbies I found joy in.

There was nothing left for me.
After all, the world could revolve without me.
My family could operate without me.
And the life I live doesn't need to exist.

Nothing.
I was nothing.
I was nothing to this world.
I was nothing to myself.

This is where I came from.
This is how far in the cave I walked,
And how dark my world got.
Only a year ago, this is where I stood.

I am not that now.
And while I am not flawless,
And I have my dark moments,
I am glad I am here.

And maybe the world can spin without me,
But I am really glad it doesn't.

And if I had left my family,
They would be devastated.
I am happy they don't have to be.

And I have my selfish moments,
But now I know,
Wanting to live isn't one.

And I have a purpose.
While my words haven't reached anyone yet,
I know they will be useful to someone,
Even if it is just to you reading or hearing this poem.

I have crawled out of the darkness,
And I will find my way out,
Again and again,
Because I am not done living yet.

I didn't know how dark my world got,
Till I had the nerve to write it all down.
I am glad that I am here,
All safe and sound.

Fuel to Burn

I hate that you're my only flame
Nothing else burns in me
Or even burns my skin like you do
Perhaps I'll find better inspiration
But for now it's only ever you.

I hate that I am you fuel,
Your dry foliage,
I allow you to burn your way
Through my head
Straight to my heart.

I have given you the crown
Ultimately the power it comes with
I can't stop you now
Because I've relinquished the title.

I should have thought about it sooner
What I was doing to me.
How fueling you
Means damaging myself.

I'll keep it in mind for the future
I'll make sure to write it down
But I think I am a lost cause
Parts with ruined instructions.

And perhaps in my next life,
I will learn from this life
And I'll make alterations
Knowing this time who I should fuel,
Because it should have never been you.

No Longer at the Bottom

It was raining while I wrote this book.
My surface was disturbed,
Perpetually bombarded by a force
I couldn't reckon with,
Truth and honesty
Reflection and redemption,
I've spent some time getting to know me
From deep within and under my sea.

Flaws I buried
Bubble of all types
They floated to my top
And in the rain they popped.

I feared what anger would do
How it controlled all of my being
But here's the thing: all emotions,
They are fleeting.
The more time I give them,
The more resources they have
To consume and destroy everything I am.
I have decided, it's me they won't have.

And complicated contradictions
Like hating and pitting bugs
They will come around in life,
And not all of them can be
Solved with a simple solution,

But sometimes,
You can kick a nasty, poor bug out of your house.

And perhaps a memory will stick around
But it is my choice to let it go.
To unstick its grippy number of legs
And let it live somewhere else.
After all it only leads me in circles
So I'll be the first to walk the other away.

Around the world will turn
And as of right now,
I could disappear and the world will still rotate,
But still, I shouldn't leave
And my feet should stay planted,
Stuck firmly on the ground.

Sometimes the past has to be home,
That way I'll always have a place to roam
But I won't be caught
Aimlessly walking without a goal
I am walking towards a new home.
And won't be stopped.

And tricky happiness,
Isn't something I can chase down,
Because further and harder I hunt it down,
The further and harder it is to find.
If I should have it, feel it,
It shall be mine someday.

My bubbles have popped
You've seen them as they float to the top.
I've allowed you to see them,
At the same time I have.
We've unpacked them together.

I have fought
Fears and beasts,
Demons and all sorts of things
I didn't think I would have the power to beat.

Imperfect me has finally taken its spot,
Right next to perfect me at the very top.
It has its time at the surface
And is not stuffed back at the bottom.

Now that the rain has stopped,
I feel lighter
Knowing now that it is not my waters,
Having to drown imperfect me,
At the deep, dark, very bottom.

Acknowledgments

As always, I have people to thank. This book would not be here if it were just me. I owe the biggest thank you's to Brandon Allen, Stephanie, Shaniese and all the other speakers at the Youth Writter's Camp. They have provided us young people a space to learn, write, and understand ourselves and emotions. Thank you to all of them for providing this much needed time and space for the youth still learning how to manage life.

Thank you to Emily, for designing the cover. It was an amazing experience getting to watch the book come to life, and it is all thanks to you and all your hard work.

Thank you to my family for listening to me talk about this book for months and never getting to read anything until now. Thank you for always encouraging and supporting all my endeavors.

To the rooms I have worked in, thank you for providing me with a quiet, safe space to work. To the Bourns Family Youth Innovation Center, I am grateful to have been able to work and learn under your roof.

Thank you to myself, who I allowed to get vulnerable enough to step into a new place with new people and create. I am grateful I took the chance to learn who I am.

Once again, thank you everyone for everything. I am truly grateful for this experience.

youthwriterspress.com

A program of Youth Writer's Camp, Inc., Youth Writer's Press exists to create a safe space where young voices are heard, valued, and amplified. We are dedicated to producing and publishing work that allows youth to share their truths with the world. Our mission is to equip the next generation of writers with the resources, confidence, and platform to turn their stories into lasting works that resound far beyond the page.

youthwriterscamp.com

This book was created as part of Youth Writer's Camp, Inc., a nonprofit organization whose mission is to motivate communities to redefine hope for young people through mentoring, enrichment, and creativity.

In our workshops and programs, we blend literacy enrichment, social-emotional development, and creative entrepreneurship — using writing as a tool for healing, growth, and community connection.

Youth Writer's Camp Values:

COURAGE Creating the strength to face challenges with confidence.

RESILIENCE Creating the ability to bounce back and keep moving forward.

EMPATHY Creating connections by truly understanding others' feelings.

AUTHENTICITY Creating a space where you can be your true self without masks.

TRANSPARENCY Creating an atmosphere of openness and honesty, where vulnerability is valued.

ENTERPRISING Creating opportunities through innovation and a dynamic mindset.

www.ingramcontent.com/pod-product-compliance
Lightning Source LLC
Chambersburg PA
CBHW070352130626
46556CB00007B/3142